DEFEATING TRAUMA

April Morris

DEDICATION

This book is dedicated to my first daughter, my baby girl, Kyleisha. Although you were just a little girl at the time, thank you for standing with me through my ups and downs. You've been with me every step of the way as I lived the message contained in the pages of this book. Your smile and your prayers carried me through some of my darkest days. You are the reason why I needed to give my life to Christ because you deserved so much more. Thank you for the times you've said, "Mommy, don't cry; it's going to be alright."

You are an overcomer! You have defeated trauma and the odds that were stacked against you. I am so proud of you. Continue to move forward. God has great things in store for you. The best is yet to come.

ACKNOWLEDGMENTS

Finding freedom from the past and hope for the future

To my Heavenly Father: Without You, I am nothing. My heart is filled with gratitude for who You are and all you have done for me. Thank You for looking beyond my faults and seeing my needs. You have given me countless chances to choose You. Thank You for shaping me and molding me; and most importantly, thank You for Your unconditional love that rescued me. My heart belongs to You. You are the Greatest Love of all!

To my Boaz, Best Friend, Lover, and confidant Vincent Morris: WOW! What can I say? Your love is amazing. You make me better in every sense of the word. I don't know where I would be without you. You are the next best thing to my Heavenly Father. God intended for you to be mine before the foundations of the world. It's amazing how His love flows through you to me. These words found in the song "Believe," by Brian C. Wilson sum up how I feel about you: "If I am dreaming; then let me die in my sleep because I don't think I could take one real minute without you in it."

Thank you for always seeing the best in me, for speaking life over me, for being my biggest fan, for cultivating me, for encouraging me to write, and for rescuing me from the burning building of life. And above all, thank you for pulling me up in the spirit and allowing Jesus to be Lord of your life. I love you to life. You are my air.

To all of my children and grandchildren. I thank God for giving me another chance to love and parent better. Thank you loving me and accepting me into your hearts. You inspire me to love unconditionally, to see and nature the beauty in each of you and to honor the responsibility with which I have been entrusted. Your love and laughter keep me moving forward.

To my beautiful mother, Martha Allen: Thank you for loving and supporting me in everything – the good, the bad, and the ugly. It is because of your support that Kylie and I survived. You are always there when I need you. You are the epitome of a Strong Black Woman. You've endured much and selflessly gave up much for those you love…especially me, your favorite! Thanks, Mom.

To my spiritual mother, Apostle Lorraine Drake: Where have you been all my life? Thank you for mothering my husband and training him in spiritual warfare and the depths of the spirit. Thank you for seeing me in the spirit and for being used by God to break the bondage of my past. God has and continues to use you in a mighty way as a mid-wife and deliverer. Your giving heart, prayers, and intercessions pulled us through some challenging times.

To all those who instructed me in the Word of God, taught me how to pray, prayed for me, and exposed me to great people of God and to a world of possibilities. I am forever grateful.

To everyone who walked with me and strengthen me on this journey. Thank you. And to everyone who supported and celebrated my promise of marriage. Your labor of love will never be forgotten.

A sincere heart of gratitude to my coach Eddie Smith and Worldwide Publishing Group, LLC. There would be no book without you. Only God could have divinely connected us in 2010 when I took your book writing course. That was the beginning of what is now Defeating Trauma. The course allowed me to create the first manuscript and to reach a level of healing that only writing could produce. I had a promise from the Lord that I would be write books but had no idea how or when it would happen. God words never comes back void. Thank you for believing in me and for pushing me when I wanted to quit.

FOREWORD

Many situations in life set us up to experience the love of Jesus. Although these "setups" tend to be very difficult and lonely seasons, God always uses them to make us whole and free. Christ loves us and wants us to be a living testimony of His ability to take the broken pieces of our life and put them back together for His glory.

Many people are bound by generational curses, past abuse, addictions, rejection, and sexual immorality. These are devices the enemy used to try to abort God's plan for Apostle April's life. She lived a life of brokenness, encountered many struggles, and made many mistakes in her pursuit of God. But her sincere desire to know Jesus in His fullness caused her to press through the crowd until she could touch the hem of His garment. There, she found the deliverance and acceptance she so desperately craved. The personal experiences she candidly writes about in this book were all steppingstones to her now fully discovered completeness in Jesus Christ.

This book will encourage and assist you in walking through the hills and valleys of your own life, ultimately helping you to become the person God has ordained you to be. Many of you will find pieces of yourself in Apostle April Morris's story, and you will also find the same hope she discovered in Christ. If you are in a broken place right now, God's love is calling you to Him. He wants to restore you into sweet fellowship with Him so you can begin the business of fulfilling your destiny. God has a plan for you and it is good. Discover what it is and start living it today!

Apostle Lorraine Drake
Founder, Jehovah Jireh & That Love Prevails Ministries
Philadelphia, PA

CONTENTS

CHAPTER 1
MY FIRST EXPERIENCE WITH TRAUMA

Too Young for the Trauma?

Trauma appeared to be a natural occurrence in my life growing up. At the age of three, we lived in North Carolina, my birthplace, where I witnessed a violent domestic altercation between my parents. My dad beat my mother with a hammer and a screwdriver; then he turned on my brother and me. Thankfully, my mother acted quickly to get us out of harm's way. Not long after that horrible night, she took us to South Carolina to live with our grandmother. It was then for the first time when I felt like I did not belong or was accepted. At the age of five, we would eventually move to Philadelphia, where the next chapter of abuse occurred.

My mother, already a single parent of five, married my stepfather in 1983, after giving birth to my youngest sister. Before having my brother and me, she had three older children from previous relationships. She opted to leave them in South Carolina to be reared by her mother and relocated to Philadelphia with my brother and me when I was five. Somewhere along the way, my birth father also moved to Philadelphia. However, my brother and I were never allowed to see him because of his violent tendencies. My mother feared for our lives.

It wasn't until I became an adult that I learned my dad suffered from severe mental illness. Due to his illness, he wasn't involved in my brother's and my life, not because he didn't want us. When this information was released to me, I was angry. I grew up mad at my dad and didn't want to be bothered with him.

I learned that when my mother was pregnant with me, my Father did not want me and tried to convince her to have an abortion. Unaware of it at the time, the trauma I suffered in my formative years, even from the womb, caused a spirit of rejection to take root in me well into adulthood. Many years later, it would take the help of the Holy Spirit and much prayer to free me from that bondage. I can see how God intervened in my life along the way because He had a plan for me.

Resentment and rejection were prevalent in my family but was never discussed growing up. It was the elephant in the room. Everyone knew it was there but ignored it. I can only imagine the pain felt by my three older siblings. They were left in South Carolina while mother reared my brother, my sister, my stepfather's two other children (my siblings), and me in Philadelphia. Our family dynamic was broken and divided.

After my mother married, our family continued to be divided in new ways. We had many good times with my new brother and sisters, but from a child's lens, it appeared to be more bad times than good. I grew up feeling mistreated, unwanted, and unloved. There were never any verbal expressions of love in our household. My parents never learned to verbalize and emotionally express love to their children. They showed love by providing our basic needs of shelter, clothing, and food. They were raised similarly by their parents and did the best they could.

Emotional neglect was not an intentional act by my parents. Most parents don't consider the emotional needs of their children. Their main focus was on meeting our basic necessities. My parent's emotional disconnect caused immediate and long-term consequences in my life. In my childhood, I suffered from low self-esteem, depression, and substance abuse. When I became an adult, more issues were added to my already childhood issues. I dealt with a lack of self-discipline, anger, aggressive behaviors, and difficulties trusting others or relying on them.

"Trauma creates changes you don't choose..."

By my late 20s, I had grown tired of my life. I was out of control and steadily spiraling downward. I was running the streets doing anything I thought I was big and bad enough to do – alcohol, drugs, sex – you name it, I was doing it. I was the poster child for women who were "looking for love in all the wrong places." I knew that none of those things that I used to numb the emptiness inside would give me what I desperately needed. I continued to spiral downward, and as a result, I was perpetually depressed and unhappy.

My promiscuous behavior in my young-adult years was the result of many years of emotional, verbal, and sexual abuse I endured as a child. As a little girl, I felt empty and full of sadness. I was fearful of dying and often cried out to God for answers about my existence. Why did He create me? I never understood the purpose of being born because my life was full of suffering at an early age. Was it merely to suffer and die?

Looking back, I realized that the sexual abuse affected my behavior in school and at home. At times, I rebelled against everyone in authority. I disrespected my teachers and family members every chance I got. I had an issue with my mouth and attitude. Correction was not handled well by me. Teachers would ask me to stop chewing gum or stop talking, and I responded with a horrible mood. I didn't talk too much at home; however, I always had something to say when I thought something was unfair. I would stomp up the stairs and slam doors. Being teased and bullied in school didn't help either until I started to fight back. I thought the only way to gain control was to become the bully, which lead to more trouble for me.

Traumatizing Events

So, here I am six-years-old in a dark, moist room with stairs. Not sure about what was happening. Are we playing hide and seek? Where is everyone else? I realized quickly that no one else was coming. That day was the beginning of years of molestation, and no one could know. It was our secret because this was family. Why would my family want to harm me? I've lived with the guilt and shame for many years because I did not want to make anyone mad. And besides, what would I say? Why would I tell? And who would believe me?

The sexual abuse was the beginning of life-altering events. Growing up was difficult. I was teased as a little girl because of my clothes, weight, hair, and dark skin. In school, kids would bully me and want to fight me for no reason. It was like I had a target on my back. In elementary school, I was tormented by one girl whose entire family went to the same school. I would run home because I was scared of them. I cried every day, hoping things would get better. I don't remember whether or not my mother understood how bad it was for me. I made excuses about being sick, hoping my mother would let me stay home, but that didn't happen.

I was tired of running and decided that I was no longer going to be bullied. The only way to stop it was to stand up to the bully and fight! So, I did. I took out all of the fears, pain, and suffering that the one girl caused me out on her with my fist, and they never bothered me again. Instead of things ending there, I became the bully and started mistreating others. Hurt people indeed hurt people even as a child.

My identity had been stolen from me before I even knew I had an identity. I felt damaged and flawed. I battled with low self-esteem because I was mistreated by people close to me. These ups and downs drastically impacted the way I saw myself. The negative self-image fueled the self-destructive decisions I made in my life. I also became suspectable to more mistreatment.

"Most bad behavior comes from insecurity."

Being around the few friends I had was great, but I was insecure in my relationships. I did not want to share my friends with anyone. I became envious of their other friends and what they had. Comparing myself to others became a part of my life. I measured myself to them, and I felt that I was inferior. I was never pretty enough or good enough for anyone. I felt alone, so I began to do things I said I would never do to get people to pay attention and to accept me. This behavior followed me well into my adult years.

CHAPTER 2
HIDDEN THINGS

At the time I was being molested, no one knew about it. I wasn't sure who to tell or how to explain what had happened. Communication was not a common practice in my family. Everyone dealt with their issues internally, on their own. So, I was wrapped in secrecy, and life continued. It wasn't until I was 30 years old when I broke the silence and told my mother. She didn't take it too well and attempted to figure out how it was possible. The shock and confusion on her face were heartbreaking. I should have told her sooner, but the guilt and shame were too unbearable.

The Effects of Secrets!

The effects of the hidden things began to manifest outwardly at age 14. My behavior was detrimental to my well-being. It was the first of the many destructive practices that I couldn't stop. It was my first time getting drunk, my first sexual intercourse encounter, and my early pregnancy.

Fourteen was a lousy year. It was the first of many times I cried out to God for His help to deliver me from my troubles, and I wouldn't do it again. Little did I know, it was just the beginning of bad choices that lead to the downward spiral to destruction.

I was being eaten alive on the inside. How did I end up addicted to alcohol, drugs, and sex? I always said I would never end up the way I saw so many others around me. The things I engaged in to escape the trauma was just a band-aid; they could never bring healing or peace to my life. I was hemorrhaging internally and didn't know it.

"There are wounds that never show on the body that are deeper and more hurtful than anything that bleeds."

Soon after my daughter's birth, I embarked upon a phase in my life where I became very ambitious and had to prove everyone wrong that said I would never amount to anything. I was determined to work to provide for my daughter and to complete high school. I began working at the age of 15 and have been working since. At that time, I was desperately trying to survive, not knowing that God's true plan for me was to be more than a conqueror and overcomer.

During my daughter's early years, I didn't consider myself a parent because I had no emotional attachment to the little girl I had brought into the world. I simply took care of her natural needs, much in the same way my parents reared my siblings and me. My time was devoted to working and school, which left her in the care of my mother 85 percent of the time.

My daughter's dad was never involved in her life. When I was pregnant, he came to me only once, vowing his support. That turned out to be a lie. We lived in the same neighborhood and would see each other often, but he had nothing to do with our daughter or me.

I got involved with another guy, and we began to live a life of an exclusive relationship like adults, but we were kids playing grown-up. We were too young for that kind of relationship, but it was accepted by our parents. I have much respect for him, and we are like family today because of the role he played in my daughter's life. He was accepting of my daughter and me and showed her the fatherly love she needed. His family was also very supportive and welcoming of us.

By the time I was 16, I was pregnant again. I couldn't believe it! Even though I was engaged in behaviors that would lead to being pregnant, I still couldn't believe it. Poor choices had become the norm. I sat in the house every day, ashamed and depressed.

My water broke when I was just five months, and I had to be rushed to the hospital. The doctors tried to save the baby by performing an emergency C-section but failed. My little boy did not survive. My boyfriend took the miscarriage very hard, but admittedly, I was relieved. I was only 16 and could not fathom having two children while I was still in high school. Soon after that, my boyfriend began to sell drugs, smoke marijuana, and engaged in relationships with other girls. He also suddenly became jealous and over-protective, even possessive. After four years, I decided to end our relationship after graduating from high school.

While all of this was going on in my life, my daughter suffered. After all, I was checked out emotionally as a mother because I didn't know how to be present. Everything I did was about me. I was a selfish person. I went from relationship to relationship, looking for love and self-worth. During those dark times, my daughter would always encourage me and let me know that everything will be alright. God has a way of winking at you when you need it the most. Unfortunately, Godwink wasn't enough to change me.

After that relationship ended, it didn't take me long to hook up with someone new. He had a girlfriend at the time, but I didn't care. The demon of lust that controlled us drew us together. We dated for about five years, but the relationship was very toxic. He was a very jealous and possessive man, to the extent that he tried to isolate me from my family and friends. He was also physically and emotionally abusive. I loved him, though, or so I thought. Every time I tried to get out of the relationship, he threatened my life. We often fought for no apparent reason and were both heavy drinkers and marijuana smokers. I found out much later that he snorted cocaine regularly, which explained his mood swings and the abuse.

At around the age of 21-23, I became pregnant with my abusive boyfriend's child. I knew I couldn't have the baby because I would have to deal with him for the rest of my life, and that was the last thing I wanted to do. So, I decided to have an abortion. While I was on the doctor's table terminating the pregnancy, I simply cried. I tried to justify the decision I had made in my mind, but nothing seemed to make sense during those moments as the life of my unborn child was being snuffed out.

I knew I desperately needed to get out of the relationship if I wanted to live. I had no idea what he was capable of doing. After mustering up the courage to leave him, the first place I headed was to church. That was the second time I promised God I would get my life together – only if He got me out of that toxic relationship alive. God was faithful to honor my request, but I did not keep up my end of the agreement. If nothing else, I knew my days of dating controlling men were over.

I began to feel like I had grown up too fast and had missed out on the fun years of my life. I was playing the wife at 15 years old. What was I thinking about! So, I began partying hard. On any given week, from Thursday to Sunday night, I could be found at bars and house parties that were overflowing with drugs, alcohol, and sex. I waged a personal war against men. I was done with being hurt by them, so I figured I would treat them like they had treated me for so many years. I began to use them for whatever I could get out of them. I was in control, or so I thought.

My girlfriends and I were the life of the party everywhere we went. Several of my girlfriends were enrolled at the same university, so I spent most of my time on their college campus on the weekends. I had an agenda, and it wasn't to get an education; I just wanted to party and have a good time. However, even when I was hanging out with the girls, I was often very depressed. I put on a façade that everything was okay and that I was living my best life. There were many days and nights I cried out for change but continued doing the things I was doing. I did not want to live the life I was living, but I did not know how to stop. It was a vicious cycle.

I knew things were really bad with me when I started to drink and smoke weed by myself several days a week. I had moved to seven different apartments in Philadelphia within eight years. There was no stability in my life. At the time, I had a good job and made decent money, but that began to fall apart, too. I even began to sleep with a married man. Although I was tired of feeling like someone's sloppy leftovers, I didn't feel like I was good enough to be anyone's Number One. I led a very dangerous lifestyle and was at my lowest during those years. It was only by the mercies of God that I did not contract HIV or AIDS. My sin, however, led to the consequences of contracting other sexually transmitted diseases, dealing with severe bouts of depression, and having very poor self-esteem.

By this point in my life, I had grown cold and emotionless. In some way or another, all of my relationships had stripped away, even the fake confidence and self-esteem I had left. I was able to suppress my feelings to the point where nothing affected me. It was as if all the craziness in my life was happening to someone else – being molested by family members, having a baby at 14, losing a baby at 16, having an abortion in my early 20s, abusive and controlling boyfriends. It all seemed like I had an out-of-body experience every single day. It would take me years later to find out how utterly deceived I was in thinking that none of those things I experienced affected me, even though I had managed to become numb to the pain. The secret faults we try to suppress or hide will eat us alive. I learned that the hard way.

CHAPTER 3
TURNING POINT

Hitting bottom

In the article "7 Famous People Who Hit Bottom—and Turned It Around," Fred Cohn tells the story of Giuseppe Verdi's lowest point.

At age 27, Giuseppe Verdi was an Italian opera composer. His second opera had been a resounding flop, closing on opening night. Far worse: over the past two years, his beloved wife and both infant children had died, victims of cholera. Despondent, Verdi became a recluse, reading trashy Victorian novels and writing, not a note. He planned to give up composing altogether. When a producer sent him the text for a proposed new Biblical opera, *Nabucco,* he threw it on the table in disgust.

Whether he was looking for it or not, at this low point of his life, a new path became visible. The composer later recalled, "The roll of paper opened out; and without knowing quite how, he found himself staring at the page in front of me, and his eyes fell on this line: 'Va Pensiero sull'ali dorati.'" ("Fly, thought, on the golden wings.")

The words were the beginning of a chorus of exiled Hebrew slaves, and they "gave Verdi a jolt: he saw the number as a metaphor for his nation's patriots, struggling to free themselves from Austrian rule. He started writing obsessively. *Nabucco* proved to be a smash, and Verdi went on to become Italy's most celebrated composer, writing works like *Aida* and *Rigoletto*. 'Va, Pensiero,' meanwhile, is a melody everybody in Italy knows by heart; in 2008, an Italian senator proposed making it the national anthem."

Everyone hits low points in life, and my day had come. My life was like a roller coaster that had its share of low points. Many of the challenges I've faced demanded a decision for change. In my heart, I knew I couldn't keep going on the way I was.

It was the fall of 1998 when I once again decided to rededicate my life to Christ. I was serious this time. I prayed that prayer again: *"God, if you do this for me, I'll serve you; If you get me out of this jam, I'll never do it again."* I cannot recall how many times I've uttered those words over the years – oh, 1, 2, 3, 4 too many times. But, this time, my heart was different, and I had a genuine desire to live for Christ.

That fall afternoon, I visited my mother when I ran into several members from a neighborhood church as they were doing their weekly street evangelism. I used to attend the church several years before but had drifted back into the world. I stopped to talk with them for a few minutes, at which time the minister asked me when I would be coming back home. That did it for me. I needed to belong somewhere, and I remembered the joy and peace I felt when I attended the church. I rededicated my life to Christ right there on the street corner.

"The ultimate turning point in our spiritual lives begins with repentance. This old-fashioned word basically means to turn—in fact, to make a complete U-turn."

Growing Pains

The change was difficult because I had to unlearn what I had allowed to take root in my heart and learn what life in Christ was. Dying to my desires was and still is never easy, but it is necessary for growth. I desperately wanted to change because I could not get out of the vicious cycle on my own. I made one bad decision after the next. My poor choices didn't only affect me, but my daughter and other family members. So, I was willing to do whatever it took to be and do better. I was relentless! No matter what came my way, I was determined to experience the peace and joy that a relationship with Jesus produced.

After I received Christ as my personal Savior, I learned the importance of godly repentance. The knowledge that God wanted my life to change for the better more than I did was life-changing in itself. In fact, He is the real source of the motivation to repent. "The Lord is not slack concerning His promise, as some count slackness, but is longsuffering toward us, not willing that any should perish but that all should come to repentance" (2 Peter 3:9).

I desperately desired change and to live a life free from the guilt and shame for the wrong things I have done. This does not mean that change is immediate and complete. Overcoming and learning to think as God thinks, is a lifelong process.

Key Components of The Journey

Soon after rejoining the church, I began to follow hard after God. I ran after Him as my life depended on it; in many ways, it did. I was so hungry for the things of God that I was literally in church every time the doors opened. I served on practically every committee there was to serve. I immersed myself in everything the ministry had to offer.

I attended weekly and monthly ministry classes. There I was introduced to teachings on finding my life's purpose, how to understand spiritual gifts and a host of other biblical truths. God was transforming me from the inside out, and it felt good. I'd never experienced love like this before, so I wanted to do everything I could to show my love for a God that so graciously reached down and rescued me from myself. For the first time in my life, my future seemed bright, and I was excited about what God was doing in and through me. Restoration had finally begun.

All my life, I felt like an outcast, and it drove me to desire to belong. It was refreshing to be around a community of people who pursued God and change.

During those years of my relentless pursuit of God, I neglected to spend the necessary quality time I should have with my daughter. By this time, she was about 9 or 10, and my lack of understanding of how to properly balance family and ministry obligations caused me to overlook many special and significant moments in her growth and development.

As I was going through my process of restoration, my daughter would often encourage and pray for me. When I cried, she would say: "Mommy, don't cry; everything is going to be alright." In hindsight, I now know that many of the things I thought God required of me back then was not what He was looking for at all. I thought He wanted me to serve the church and my leaders, but maybe I was just supposed to be a good mother to Kylie. It took too long for me to figure out what my priority was, and it cost me dearly. My relationship with my daughter was shattered as a result. It would be many years later, and after many difficulties that God would restore our relationship.

To the single parent, please do not take the importance of spending quality time with your children lightly. Make them a priority. Your children are a gift from God and should be treated as such. Neglected time with them is not something you can ever get back. Gifts and money cannot be used as substitutes for your love. Your children need you. You can still run hard after the Lord without missing crucial periods in your children's growth and development. They need your guidance, your time, your re-assurance when they are fearful, and the comfort your presence provides. They need to know that you will never allow anything to happen to them. They need to be safe and heard.

Experiencing Loneliness

Facing loneliness head-on was a necessary part of my process. As I abandoned everyone and everything to pursue Christ, I learned the truth about loneliness and its causes. It came as no surprise that the root of it was from the trauma of my past. A lack of meaningful connections contributed to my loneliness. God's plan for humanity is for us to be in a relationship with Him and with others. I believe there is a void in everyone that can only be filled by God. Knowing this now helped me to understand that I was expecting people to fill God's place in my life.

"Jesus said unto him, Thou shalt love the Lord thy God with all thy heart, and with all thy soul, and with all thy mind. This is the first and great commandment. And the second is like, unto it, Thou shalt love thy neighbor as thyself." Matthew 22:37-39

Loneliness is a universal human emotion that is both complex and unique to each individual. Loneliness causes people to feel empty, alone, and unwanted. Lonely people crave human contact, but their state of mind makes it more challenging to connect with other people. According to many experts, loneliness is not necessarily about being by yourself. Instead, it's a state of mind.

There were many times that I felt lonely despite being surrounded by family and friends, roommates, and other peers. Loneliness was a struggle for me during my childhood and early walk with the Lord. Low self-esteem and lack of confidence in myself often lead me to believe that I was unworthy of other people's attention. My battle with loneliness and depression kept me pursuing God with all my heart for change. I longed for the peace and joy that Christ provided. I never stop seeking God's goodness and deliverance.

Renewing My Mind

My mind was full of negative thoughts. I was a pessimist about everything and never thought good things would happen to me. I needed to learn how to stop being negative about everything. The more negative I was the more negative outcomes and things I attracted. I think this was by far the most challenging part of my journey. Learning what the Word of God said about me helped me form affirmations that I memorized and confess over myself.

CHAPTER 4
DELIVERANCE IS FREEDOM

Deliverance

Deliverance is a must in a believer's life. Without it, the believer would be bound by the past, not able to follow Jesus. To me, the simple definition of deliverance is being rescued and set free from bondage caused by demonic entities that oppress and controls a person's life through their mind, will, and emotions. I believe that there are many stages to deliverance. The process, however, starts with accepting Jesus as personal Savior. Jesus came for the broken, sick, and lost.

"The Spirit of the Lord is upon Me because He hath anointed Me to preach the Gospel to the poor. He hath sent Me to heal the brokenhearted, to preach deliverance to the captives, and recovering of sight to the blind, to set at liberty them that are bruised." Luke 4:18

Listed below are key areas to consider and understand when thinking about deliverance.

- Inner healing is the deep-level healing work of Jesus Christ for the whole person. It includes addressing the brokenness of painful events, suppressed memories, unforgiveness of others, debilitating depression, and personal condemnation. Healing by biblical counseling establishes self-worth on a believer's identity in Christ, his presence in all life circumstances, and his power to set a captive sinner free. Replace damaging thoughts and feelings with truth, the mindset of Christ, and his unconditional love.

- Spiritual Warfare is the ongoing fight to resist Satan, and his fallen angels' evil works in the invisible world as they try to thwart God's purposes and oppress humans in the visible world. It is not a battle for power but an active engagement of enforcing the authority of Christ upon demons. Warfare includes strategic encounters with both higher-level spirits overseeing spiritual realms, territories, and institutions and lower-level demons afflicting individuals through the world's mindset, the sinful nature, and by direct attacks of the devil's demons themselves.

- Stronghold is a designate area where the enemy Satan still has some control over a person's life. This control may stem from a pattern of ongoing sin, an external attack by a demonic spirit, or the internal attachment to a part of the body, mind, will, or emotions. Bondage to spiritual strongholds are broken foremostly through repentance, prayer, obedience, and embracing Christ's truth and power to set a person free. Strongholds that carry demonic attachment requires a more profound inner healing ministry and even deliverance.

The Need to Be Delivered

Disappointment is the failure of an expectation. Over the years, I had my fair share of losses. Each year of my life, I gathered and carried more baggage created by my past, failed relationships, and unrealistic expectations of others. It took me years to figure out that I couldn't fix myself. I believed the lie that I told myself that I needed to be changed before committing my way to the Lord. I was wrong again. Every time I wanted to do what was right, I managed to do what was wrong. Something was hindering me from walking in victory, but I had no clue about what it was.

I finally decided that enough was enough and admitted that I needed help. I knew I couldn't do it on my own. Walking down the path of self was leading me to destruction fast. After accepting the gift of salvation, submission to God's Word became vital to the journey to freedom. The Word of God showed me my position in Christ, but my mind needed to be renewed. My belief system needed to change. God began to root out the things the world taught me and prepared my heart to learn His ways.

The process was and continues to be challenging, but it's necessary. Every part of the old life that died was painful because it was a stripping away of everything I ever knew. God is a strategist, and He knows what to deal with and when. I remember sitting in the church crying out from within, "can anybody see me"? Something is wrong, and I don't know what it is.

The dangerous lifestyle I lived before Christ rescued me altered who I was created to be. I dealt with the consequences of contracting sexually transmitted diseases, having an abortion, rejection, dealing with severe bouts of depression, low self-esteem, and being bound by the guilt and shame of it all.

Although it was frightening, I had to become willing to give it all to God. The devil could no longer hold it over my head and torment me when I mustered up the courage to expose my sin. God reveals to heal. Things I had hidden began to surface—nothing I've done or could ever do surprises God. I could no longer make excuses for my issues and shortcomings.

Deliverance Requires Forgiveness

Blaming others for my state of stuck was not cutting it. Forgiving myself and others was one of the hardest things I faced, but I had to do it. The Bible tells me that if I don't forgive, my Heavenly Father will not forgive me. That was not an option for me. All I wanted at that point was to make God proud. I needed to be accepted and loved. Understanding that God accepted me because of His love for me and not by what I did was profound.

Deliverance began that day in 1998, when I admitted that my life was a wreck, and I asked Jesus to come into my heart. I believe there are levels of deliverance. That first step changed the course of my life. The more I learned of God, the more I became aware of my issues. I began to accept the fact that I was broken and that I had life all wrong.

I served in ministry; some would say faithfully and with joy. If anyone was looking for me, they could find me at church doing whatever needed to be done. I even preached a few sermons, but there were still wars raging within me. I vowed to refrain from sexual sin until I was married. I learned that I could start over again, but my past's secret faults opened a door of perversion that manifested in masturbation and kept me in bondage because I was too ashamed to confess my struggles to anyone. As unusual as it seems, I prayed someone would see that I was still so messed up. I needed help!" I was too fearful to admit my struggles, so I continued to serve in ministry and tried to deal with the skeletons in my closet on my own. That was the worst thing I could have ever done. I did more serving than seeking God and became very good at pretending I had it all together. This attitude eventually caused me to engage in more sin.

The enemy began to torment my mind with lies and accusations of being a failure and a disappointment to God and my leaders. The bondage and oppression became so intense I was able to feel bound and constrained. It was around May 2006. I was home in my room, crying out for God's help, but was unable to move. Trying to shake free was extremely difficult and frustrating. I knew something had me, but I couldn't shake free from it. I felt a strong demonic presence attack me. I screamed: "Get off of me!" Immediately, the demonic presence lifted, and I fell to my knees and cried out for God to save me. In that instant, I felt the presence of God enter the room, and felt His love and compassion. My deliverance began that day. It was yet another turning point in my life. It would be the day that was the catalyst for the path I am on today.

Results of Deliverance

My life was changing for the better; however, it appeared to go from me being strong, independent and making things happen to weak and needy. What in the world was happening? I wasn't expected that. God was teaching me I wasn't alone, and that I wasn't meant to do life by myself. Deliverance helped me realize that everyone was not out to abuse me. I no longer needed to please people to prove that I am valuable.

Deliverance has done so many things for me that I will only list a few in hopes that my salvation and what God can and is desiring to do in your life will help you submit to the process of breaking free. Because of deliverance:

- I Have been set free from sin and death.

- I know who I am in Christ.

- I have a voice

- I no longer seek to please men.

- Stability of mind

- I can love others

- No longer have a hard heart of unforgiveness.

- I can make the right decisions

- Fear no longer controls my life

- No longer suffer from depression

- Free from guilt and shame

- Free from being a perfectionist

- Free from ungodly ambition

Deliverance is a Process

The truth of the matter is that every believer will go through deliverance until Jesus returns. There are some unresolved issues that we have no idea that requires attention, but God knows. And as I stated before, He is a strategist. He knows when it is time to bring to light what's hidden to walk in another freedom level. I am an advocate for deliverance because I understand the significant impact on an individual's life.

CHAPTER 5

FINDING HOPE!

In the fall of 2003, I attended a service at a sister church where the pastor invited a prophet to minister for several nights. The buzz was that the man of God was a "true prophet," a person who is chosen by God to speak for Him through divine inspiration. That evening, another young lady and I were assigned to accompany our pastor to the service. I couldn't wait to get there!

As I listened to the prophet's message on the ministry gift of prophecy, I couldn't help but wonder what God had in store for me that night. The teaching was clear and easy to understand, and I was grateful he took the time to debunk much of the mystery surrounding this particular ministry gift. When he finished teaching, he opened himself up to be used by God to prophesy over those in attendance.

As I listened to him speak prophetically over the people's lives, I quietly prayed that God would use him to talk to me. I noticed it was getting late, and he seemed to be getting ready to wrap up. Then, it happened. The prophet looked straight at me and asked for my name, as was his standard way of preparing to relay a prophetic message from the Lord. He then began: *"April, April, you know what April...the Lord told me to tell you that you are not going to be alone. He was going to send you Boaz."* And that was only the beginning! The things God had spoken through the Prophet to me that night blew me away. Based on the biblical account of Ruth, I knew that Boaz was a wealthy man. He secretly observed the widowed Moabite Ruth as she gleaned corn in his field to provide for her and her mother-in-law, Naomi, one of his distant relatives. Ruth found favor in Boaz's sight because she was a woman of worth. In the end, Boaz redeemed both Ruth and Naomi from a life of poverty by taking Ruth as his wife [Ruth 3 – 4:13]. Well, I couldn't wait to meet my Boaz!

That night, the prophet also told me to get my check-list out and review it. This "check-list" was a written list of attributes I desired my husband to have. Ladies, if you don't already have one, start compiling your check-list. I discuss the importance of the list in a later chapter. There was no way the man of God could have possibly known about my check-list and many of the other things he shared with me that night, so I knew it was from the Lord.

The prophetic word gave me hope. It let me know that God cared about me, even after all the wrong I'd done in my life. I was encouraged, but I was also amazed by God's love. I never imagined those beautiful things God said to me that night could happen for me. Stuff like that only happened in the movies.

Nevertheless, I hid those words in my heart. At the end of the service, I received a tape recording of my prophetic word. I can't tell you how grateful I was to have that recording for the countless times doubt and discouragement tried to paralyze me in the many years it took before my promise of marriage was fulfilled.

If you receive a prophetic word, please find out if it was recorded and request a copy. At the very least, write down what was said to you immediately after. You're going to need it! I played my tape so much that I'm surprised it hasn't fallen apart. Several promises were spoken over my life that night in 2003 that I'm waiting to see manifest.

That experience with the prophet taught me the importance of being in a Bible-believing church where spiritual gifts are in operation. If I hadn't been under a ministry that understood the prophetic gift, I would not have experienced such a powerful and life-changing word from God that night. I began to learn the importance of spiritual gifts operating in the local church and the Body of Christ at large. These gifts are necessary for believers to realize their full potential in God.

After receiving that word concerning marriage, people thought I had become desperate and crazy, but I didn't care. I rehearsed it over my life day and night. Just about every Friday night during our weekly corporate prayer services, I would pray for my future husband and all the other single women's husbands. I was determined to continue praying and believing God until my change came.

CHAPTER 6

HOW I LEARNED CONTENTMENT

A farmer complained about the lake on his property that always needed to have the fish thinned out. The rolling hills made it more difficult for him to run the fence rows. Sometimes he couldn't even see his cows because they had so much territory to cover. At night it was so dark it was hard to walk from the barn back to his house.

He decided to sell the place and move somewhere really nice. He called a real estate agent and made plans to sell his property. A few days later, he picked up the local paper, looking for a new place to live. His eye caught an ad for a lovely country home in an ideal location – quiet and peaceful.

It had soft rolling hills, a pristine lake stocked with bass, a classic barn surrounded by natural flowers and soft grass, and came complete with a beautiful herd of Black Angus cows. It was just close enough to a small town convenient but far enough out to be uncluttered by city lights, traffic, and noise.

He read the ad a second and then a third time before realizing the real estate agent had given her a description of the place he currently owned. He called her and told her to cancel the ad. He said, "I've changed my mind. I've been looking for a place like that all my life."

Just like the farmer, I needed a new perspective on my circumstances to understand that my life as a single woman wasn't as bad as I had believed.

Learned contentment

My first trip to Ghana, West Africa, in 2003 had a tremendous impact on my perspective. I thought my life was full of suffering until I witnessed the despair and living conditions of Africans. Many people lived in concrete houses with no doors or windows. There were villages where there was no running water or electricity, and they used the same water that they deposited waste in and bathed in to cook. Children were working carrying heavy baskets of merchandise on their heads to help buy food and necessities. I was heart-broken. I realized that I needed to be grateful for all the things I had and the opportunities afforded to me.

As I continued to grow, God revealed that contentment was more than being satisfied with what I had and where I was at that moment in time.

My faith began to grow as I sought God in His Word and prayer. I learned that true contentment came from trusting Jesus Christ and confident that what I needed was in Him. Seeking the Lord with-out idols standing in my way became my way of life. The more I learned of God, the more I realized that I could not do anything apart from Him.

After I encounter the love of Jesus through repentance, I immediately resolved to wait on the Lord. I was no longer taking matters into my own hands because they always ended up wrong. My focus was on complete healing and restoration in my life. I desperately needed my relationship with the Lord to be restored. My pursuit of knowing the Lord more deeply and intimately began. I took Mary's position, who decided to sit at the Lord Jesus' feet to get the needful things that would not be taken away from her.

Dear sister, please don't get so caught up with doing the church's work, as Martha did in Luke 10:41-42, that you neglect the upkeep of your spiritual life. Make sure you take the time to feed your spirit with the Word of God, as Mary did in Luke 10:39, 42. Mary sat at Jesus' feet and learned from Him when He visited their home. Ensure that your lamps are filled and trimmed like the Five Wise Virgins, highlighted in Matthew 25:1-13. You don't want to be like the Five Foolish Virgins who were not prepared for the Bridegroom and could not get into the banquet hall when he arrived. In other words, always ensure that you have a genuine relationship with God. If you have to resign from certain groups, positions, and organizations at church or in your professional life to shore up your relationship with God, do it. It's worth it.

Waiting

Waiting can be a challenge when you don't understand the purpose of it and what is developing. There were battles I still faced as I waited on the Lord. In the wars, I learned how to fight in the spirit using the word of God. When I felt discontent, worry, or doubtful, I went to the scripture; Philippians 4:6-9 until the battle ceased as I mediated on good things. I reminded myself about the suffering I witnessed in Africa.

The experience changed my perspective. Serving the Lord looked very different after significant deliverance. The way I perceived things shifted. I viewed God as a loving Father who reached for me when I fell versus a Master who was disgusted when I error. I worked while I waited and completed my bachelor's degree and developed a single's ministry.

The single's ministry helped singles understand that they had value and that it was okay to desire a spouse, but that's not the end prize. Being without a companion is a time to cultivate oneself by developing a deeper relationship with God, learning, and exploring new things. Most people suffer from a lack of identity, so God uses this time to make his sons and daughters whole.

The church can use some work learning how to minister to single individuals. Many emphases on marriage are a blessing, but being single is looked at like a plague. I've known singles, including me, that felt second-rate or less than those married. Singles were encouraged to serve, and married folks didn't have to do anything for the Lord where I went to church.

I believe that singleness is a state of mind that every born-again believer should have. The Bible declares in Philippians 2:5, "Let this mind be in you, which was also in Christ Jesus." We must submit to the work of the Holy Spirit that will produce the following desires.

1. To look more like Christ
2. To seek His will
3. To help point people to Christ
4. To live out our God-given calling
5. To rely on the sufficiency of God.
6. To develop a thankful attitude.
7. To trust Him
8. To reject fear

Time was wasted when I lacked the mind of Christ. Years of playing the comparison game kept me focused and envious of what others had. This behavior caused me to forfeit growth, joy, and peace, and delayed goals and aspirations.

CHAPTER 7
DON'T SETTLE FOR LESS

Tempted to Settle for The Status Quo

Many years passed after I received the prophetic word regarding marriage. I continued to serve the Lord; however, I began to get a little weary. I began to see other people being blessed by God in many areas. I began to play the comparison game, and, in my opinion, the people that appeared to be getting blessed didn't love God or serve Him as I did. Everyone could see that I was the super Christian, but was I wrong. I began to ask God, why was I still suffering, when was my turn coming. I thought God was taking too long, so I took matters into my own hands and made the mistake of choosing the wrong person.

"Don't settle. It's better to face a little loneliness now than a lifetime of loneliness with the wrong person." – Mandy Hale

Deceived

In November of 2005, as I was preparing for a medical mission trip to Ghana, West Africa, my life took a spiritual nosedive. I experienced a spiritual TKO by the enemy. A few months prior, in September, I became involved in a relationship that initially began as a good friendship. This man and I hit it off right away, so we almost immediately began spending a lot of time together. I must mention that my faith began to waver because I thought God had forgotten about me. How could God love me, and I still was struggling in so many areas? Everything began to fall apart. I could barely afford to pay my rent and bills. I stopped giving my tithes and offerings because I didn't have enough money to take care of my little family.

This guy showed up right when I questioned everything about my faith. My lack of trust and patience blinded me from the truth. Red flags and alarms were warning me of the impending danger, but I kept turning off the alarm because I wanted to remain asleep. He was carnal minded. He believed that it was okay to live according to our fleshly desires. I tried to take a stand for what I believed to be right, but I eventually brought into the lies.

The unthinkable happened – I became sexually involved with him. I thought I was delivered from sexual temptation, but I was sadly mistaken. This taught me that avoiding a particular temptation doesn't mean deliverance from it has taken place.

Before meeting this man, I had been celibate for several years, but I still struggled with masturbation during that time. After my first sexual encounter with him, I repented and tried my best to fight off the intense sexual desire that seemed to be consuming me. A month passed, and I was able to get back on track spiritually, but it wasn't long before the devil would bring back the temptation, and I would fall for his bait and switch again. After a while, I felt helpless in controlling my sexual urges with my new friend, so I tried to seduce him into marrying me. I erroneously believed marriage would right the wrong I was doing.

My improper relationship with him went on for a few months until I realized he would not be my husband; he didn't want me; he only wanted to fulfill his lustful desires. It took me a while to figure it out, but I finally saw he was a counterfeit! The devil used him to try to sabotage my destiny, and I almost let it happen. I believe my participation in sexual sin was a direct result of the door of masturbation I had never closed. Because I was never delivered from it, the devil had a foothold on me, and he was patiently waiting for the right opportunity to take me out.

I realized that living in sin was not the plan of God for my life. The Holy Spirit was telling me that God's plan for me was greater and that I was valuable.

No matter how other Christians around me lived, I knew my path was different. I desired to live a life that pleased God. So, I cried out for help, and I kept crying out until He showed up and provided another way of escape. The relationship ended when I stopped answering his calls for pleasure. No more lies, no more sexual sin, no more settling for the counterfeit! I set my eyes on the Lord and resolved in my heart to wait on God no matter how long it took.

While You Wait

You may find yourself tempted to get in a hurry to be in a relationship. This temptation will lead you to make a quick decision about the wrong person. Remember, this is a time of cultivating yourself to maximize your full potential. You should be whole and able to bring some substance to the table when the right person arrives. By now, you know I love a good list. So, here is one of the things to consider doing while you wait on God.

- Spend time with God in His Word

- Feed your faith and starve your doubts

- Journal your journey

- Serve by helping others in need.

- Learn a new hobby

- Take yourself to dinner and a movie.

- Read good books

- Exercise

CHAPTER 8
NOT FORGOTTEN

After I got serious about giving my life to Christ, I still faced many challenges. Some were implications to the decision that I've made, and some were just the vicissitudes of life. There were so many areas that I desired to change according to the Word of God. It seemed like the more that I desired changed, the worst my life became. You know what they say, it gets worse before it gets better. I found some truth in that; however, there was a purpose in the worst. I thought, man, if I knew coming to Christ would be this bad, I would have kept living the way I was. That was my emotions speaking. Even during my wilderness process, my life was better in Christ.

Did the evangelist lie? I am 100% sure that they said Jesus was going to make everything all right! I have to admit that they never said when the all right was going to happen. The desire for a quick change fueled my pursuit for God. I've learned quickly that my timetable was slightly different than His, and still is. Delay in God's promises does not mean denial. God knew what was best for me. He had a plan that was greater than I could have ever imagined. It's funny now looking back at how I thought I knew more than God. I was wrong about that too. He was more interested in cleaning me up from the inside out than providing a quick fix that would not have lasted.

Where is God

Home Alone is a classic Christmas movie that my family watches every year. The movie is about a large family that is taking a Christmas vacation to France. The family's house is full of chaos the day they leave for vacation, and the parents accidentally leave the youngest son home alone. I am glad that our heavenly Father does not leave us during our chaos.

God has a large family that lives in a world full of chaos and confusion but has never left His children behind. God will leave the 99 to go after the one who was lost. Even with this knowledge, life still has a way of challenging that fact.

Many times, in my walk, I thought God had forgotten me. I became wearied when I didn't see a change in some key areas of my life. The internal work was happening, and I could identify the difference, but the pain of change did not appear to be a blessing to me. God is sovereign, and there was nothing that I experienced that He did not understand. When I cried out to the Lord often for help and deliverance, he heard me. He would speak to me through His Word or His children, and it encouraged me to keep pressing forward. Eventually, as time passed, those constant reminders that God was there became blurred.

I am not Forgotten

Wars were raging inside me that wanted me to quit, but I had come too far to give up. I was determined to see the goodness of the Lord. Even after taking matters into my own hands and backsliding, I experience God's unconditional love in a way I never known. He still chose me to be His daughter. The encounter of redemption that I felt at that moment was priceless. The Father's forgiveness experience changed my heart, and I knew I was different this time. I resolved to trust and wait on the Lord no matter how long He saw fit to manifest His promises for my life.

He was always there

God remained faithful when I was not faithful. And His faithfulness and love towards me sparked a new relationship between us. I became sold out. No matter what came my way or how painful it would be, I am never looking back—the cross before me and my past behind me. Today, I know that even when I don't feel Him, He is there. In His Word, he said that He would never leave me or forsake me, and I believe that with all my heart. He has proven Himself to be a Man of His Word. As the seasoned saints would say, I know too much about Him for you to make me doubt Him.

CHAPTER 9

TRUE LOVE IS WORTH THE WAIT

Blindness

What is love? That was a question I asked myself many times. I was consistent in my search for meaning. Most of my seeking led to poor decisions that caused me and those closet to me many heartaches. I needed people to accept me, and the only way I knew how to do that was to be what everyone wanted me to be. Boy, that was exhausting! I had no idea who I was or what I was to become. What's sad is that if you don't know who you are, there is always someone available to give you an identity suitable for them.

Growing up with a traumatic past, without my father and with an erroneous perception about love drove me to seek love in all the wrong places. When I began to learn about God's love, I knew I had missed it. It was tough to understand that anyone, let alone God loved me; The Creator of everything. I didn't think God cared for me at all because of all the suffering I had gone through, the insecurities, and low self-esteem. My thoughts about love were faulty.

How He Found Me

Jesus showed up for me when I was lost and broken. He received me and showered His love upon me when I was at my absolute worst. I was on my knees sobbing with a surrendered heart to do His will when I realized that God's gift of love was freely given to me. It took me a long time to believe it because of my perspective about love and acceptance. I learned that perfection could never earn His love. To experience God's love for me at that moment was life-changing. I knew nothing I did deserve it because I was lost in my mistakes.

My idea of love was erroneous. I thought I had to allow men to have sex with me to earn their love. My life consisted of pleasing people. I was deceived into thinking I had to be what everyone needed me. I wanted to be perfect, which was impossible. I pretended most of my life and lost myself. My identity was based on who I was around at the moment. Who I had become was far from my true identity.

I still had many issues and uncertainties in my life when I met Vincent. The one thing I was sure about was my relationship with Jesus and my road to recovery. My mind was being renewed from childhood trauma, yet he was interested in getting to know me. He was attracted to my spirit first and not my body. I was shocked. I must admit that I was a little offended by his words because I thought my body was the best thing about myself.

Understanding Gods love

Because I longed to be loved, I was seeking it out. So, I never intentionally rejected God's love. However, a lack of understanding about it kept me distant from Him even when I wanted to draw close. One of the ways He taught me His love for me was through the lens of Vincent's eyes, which was quite refreshing.

I wanted the man that God had for me to be an image of Him and His love. The Bible says we have not because we ask not [James 4:2]. I wanted to have everything important to me in a spouse, so I asked for it in prayer, and I created a check-list. From the very beginning, God began to show me He had fulfilled most, if not all, of the things on my list in Vincent. His attributes and behaviors were closely aligned with the Character of Christ.

"God is going to send you someone who will constantly remind you who God is," — Kim Brooks.

In the next few pages, I have included specific examples where God began to show me that Vincent was "The One" I had been waiting for all my life.

#1. **Worshipper:** One day, Vincent and I were sitting in his truck talking about various worship songs and worship artists we liked. I told him I liked Marvin Sapp, and he asked if I knew the song, "You Alone Are God," one of Pastor Sapp's biggest hits. We began to sing the song to each other. It was precious. Vincent was a worshipper and not ashamed to sing praises to our God. I desired a mate who was not ashamed to worship God.

#2. **Protector:** About two weeks after I met him, right before we began our courtship, I informed Vincent of my transportation situation. The car license plate and registration became suspended because I couldn't afford to keep up with my insurance payments when I was unemployed earlier that year. Without a second thought, he gave me his truck to drive, refusing to allow me to be on the bus in the cold. Look at God; this was evidence he was a protector, something I wanted in a husband.

#3. **Provider**, I was accustomed to being an independent single parent, but there was a time I needed some money to take care of a particular financial obligation and did not have the funds. I was afraid to ask Vincent for help, but I worked up enough courage to ask him if I could borrow the money. He was agitated that I would ask him to borrow money because he had already made it clear that whatever he had was mine. We went to his bank that day and added my name to all of his accounts, giving me full access to funds whenever I needed them. He turned all of his finances over to me. Now you know *that* was God! This act of generosity showed me Vincent was a provider, and I wanted that in a husband.

#4. It was almost Christmas of 2006, and Vincent asked me what I wanted for my gift. I needed my hair styled, but the style I wanted was very costly. When I told him what I wanted, he went straight to the bank and gave me the money. This occurred a few days before he added me to his bank accounts.

#5. Vincent accepted my daughter like she was his own. He always made sure she had everything she needed during her senior year in high school. From fees, special projects, and class trips, Vincent ensured that Kylie was well cared for.

As you can see, most of the previous accounts had to do with money and him providing for me. Vincent's actions were clear indications of how he felt about me and how serious he was about our relationship. Matthew 6:21 states, ***"For where your treasure is, there your heart will be also."*** I had his heart, and there was nothing he wouldn't do for my daughter and me. However, there were other vital ways Vincent proved his love for me.

#6. When my daughter had taken ill, Vincent was there – warring in the spirit and interceding for her while praying for me and strengthening me. Every time visitation hours were available at the facility where my daughter was admitted, he was right there. He never left our side.

#7. Vincent made me better in every sense of the word. I'd written on my check-list that I wanted a man who understood the importance of tithing and giving offerings and who was faithful in doing so.

For many years, I had given tithes and offerings faithfully; however, my offerings were very minimal because of my limited finances as a single parent. Vincent has a very giving heart, and he gave to God liberally and cheerfully. He challenged me to stretch myself when it came to offerings. I was comfortable with giving offerings to my local church and to people God placed on my heart. I thought I was doing something big with the $20 offerings I was giving at the time. Don't get me wrong, I was blessed to be able to donate that amount, but God was calling me higher in that area. I began to sow above what I could see in the natural, and I never lacked anything.

#8. Vincent was very supportive of my commitments to the Lord and my local church. I held several roles on committees, including the pastor's assistance, which meant there was always something going on at the church or related to the church that I was required to attend. As long as it didn't conflict with his church obligations, Vincent was there to support me. He would often clean the church with me on the weekends I was scheduled and attend services with me as I traveled with my pastor. He cheered me on in whatever I did. If I had a speaking engagement, he was my "Amen Corner." If no one said "Amen," I could count on his thunderous approval from the front row.

God blew my mind with Vincent. What was happening to me was much like my favorite movies *Maid in Manhattan, Brown Sugar,* and *Love and Basketball,* but ten times better. God had written the script! There was no drama, no second-guessing, and no stress. **Proverb 10:22 states, *"The blessing of the LORD, it maketh rich, and he addeth no sorrow with it."***
Vincent is my 'sorrow-less' blessing from God. It touches me every time I think about it. God is so amazing, and His love for me is overwhelming. There is nobody like Him! He blessed me with His very best when He gave me everything I prayed for in Vincent. If I knew He would be that detailed, I would have asked for a few more things.

CHAPTER 10

PROMISE FULFILLED

In July of 2006, God miraculously opened a door of employment for me at one of Philadelphia's largest governmental agencies. It was now mid-November, and I was on my standard morning routine for what I thought would be another typical workday. I'd left home to head downtown to my office at the usual time. I'd boarded the same bus and train that I took every day. When I arrived at work, I was met with all the familiar challenges that came with the job. There was nothing particularly different about that day until lunchtime.

I had walked over to a little convenience store minutes from my office to purchase lunch, as I'd done many times before. When it was my turn at the register, I noticed the soft drink I was holding appeared to have been dropped. I asked the cashier if I could quickly grab another bottle, at which time I heard a masculine voice behind me playfully offer to purchase another blouse for me if the soda were to explode on me. I turned, smiled, thanked him, grabbed another soft drink, bought my items, and quickly exited the store. Whoa! That man was *handsome!* I knew I had to pull myself together because I was very careful not to entertain any lustful thoughts since my deliverance earlier that summer. I decided then, and there I wouldn't give him a second thought. But boy was he good looking! It didn't take me long after that day to recognize that what I thought as an innocent chance meeting at a small convenience store was a "Divine Hookup" that would change the course of my life forever. In His Providence, God had a plan for me, and He set it in motion earlier that summer when I purposed to submit my life to Him, no matter the cost. That is all God wants from us, from you, a complete "Yes," and you will begin to see Him miraculously move in your life.

To my pleasant surprise, the very next day, I ran into "The Handsome Stranger" at lunchtime again. This time, I was headed to catch the train to a shoe repair shop downtown. We were on opposite sides of the gate that enclosed the parking lot attached to my office building. I knew we worked for the same company, but not in the same building. Weeks before our encounter in the convenience store, I remembered seeing him outside my office building talking with my general manager as I was leaving work for the evening. As I said good night to my boss and walked by, "The Handsome Stranger" and I briefly glanced at each other, and I felt his eyes follow me across the street as I headed to the subway.

So, as I was on my way to the shoe repair shop, "The Handsome Stranger" recognized me and said hello. I stopped, and we formally introduced ourselves to each other. His name was Vincent. I asked if he usually offered to purchase new blouses for all the women he met, playfully referring to his generous offer the day before. He responded: "No, I try the spirit by the Spirit." I couldn't believe my ears. Was this another one, 'super-spiritual,' religious guy that was willing to use Christianese language to get want he wanted? I was immediately disappointed. I could not deal with another of his kind. I've had my fair share of them and did not want to go there again. We stood at the gate and talked a bit about our faith and where we attended church—ultimately discovering that our churches fellowshipped together.

I only had an hour for lunch to get to the shoe store and back. Vincent offered to take me, and I accepted, after a moment of debate. Then I thought, what was I doing? I don't even know this man.

I remembered seeing him during a fellowship service. A friend of mine leaned over to me and asked me if I knew who the new guy was that visited the church. I wasn't interested in learning who he was. The Lord just rescued me from Satan's' plan of destruction.

We finally got back to the office. Vincent began to pray and prophesy over me. The things the Lord spoke to me was confirmation and yet hard to swallow. It was the first time God exposed the issue of my heart. At first, I was offended. Who does this man think he is calling *me* rebellious? Excuse me, Mr. Prophet, but you don't know why I did not want to answer the call of God on my life. You have no idea what I have gone through. I just wanted to go to church, sit in the pew, and be a good girl.

I kindly thanked him for the ride and hurried back to my office. About a week later, I started to think about him strongly. He had some medical problems that God brought him through. I had to check on him to make sure he was okay, but I didn't know much about him or what department he worked in. I only knew his first name, so; I asked a few people that knew him for his last name. Everyone was trying to figure out why I was looking for him because he was a big shot at the company. Instead of getting into any discussion with them, I played it cool went to the mailroom to look for his last name on the mailbox.

His last name was Morris. I sent him a message through an internal messaging system at work. At first, he acted like he didn't know who I was. I proceeded to help him regain his memory. After that interaction, we began to communicate daily.

Vincent asked me to accompany him to the office Christmas party on December 14. As much as I wanted to go with him, I couldn't because I had already invited two church members to be my guests. Dang! But I couldn't wait to see him there.

Friday, December 14, had arrived, precisely two weeks after meeting him in that convenience store, something happened. I can't say I knew for sure what would happen that night; I just knew I had to see him. He was already at the party when I called to let him know I was on my way. To my surprise, he informed me that he was getting ready to leave to attend the weekly Friday night prayer services at his church. "Ohmigosh," I thought, "he couldn't leave before I got there!" I asked him to wait until I arrived, and thankfully, he agreed. Looking back, I think his attempt to leave was just his sweet way of trying to appear macho; he was very good at doing that.

When I arrived at the party, we spotted each other from across the room and everything stood still. It felt like something out of a movie. You know, those romantic love scenes from *Brown Sugar* or *Maid in Manhattan*? The stuff I thought would never happen to me Yes, it was just like that. And it was happening.

As festive holiday music wafted through the speakers in the ballroom, everything seemed to move in slow motion. It took forever for us to reach each other that night. The way Vincent was being pulled in every direction by many of our colleagues, you would have thought he was a celebrity. Finally, we were standing face to face. I introduced him to my guests, and they went off to enjoy the party. We tuned everything and everyone around us out. I saw it in his eyes, and I knew it was real. He made me feel pleasantly remarkable. Nothing could distract him from me. His mouth uttered phrases like, "You are beautiful." And His eyes spoke even louder.

The time must have flown by because before I knew it, the party was ending, and we were standing outside, coatless, in the middle of December. Perhaps it was the warmth of Vincent's gaze that made that wintry night seem like a beautiful summer's evening. We had only talked for about 30 minutes, but it could have easily been forever. Is this what eternity feels like?

The clock struck 10, and we reluctantly said our goodbyes. Vincent left before I did to make it to prayer service, as he was very committed to the Lord and weekly church attendance. I left shortly after that and headed to prayer services at my church. On the short drive to church, I wondered what had just happened between us. I couldn't figure it out, but I knew that it was different than anything I had ever experienced before, and I liked it. I liked him.

Vincent and I almost immediately began spending lots of time together soon after that night at the office Christmas party. One day as we sat talking in my apartment, he informed me that God had told him I would be his wife. As he spoke, I thought to myself, "What in the world is he talking about?" We'd only known each other for what seemed like 10 minutes! But, seriously, at that point, it had only been about two weeks since we'd met. Shouldn't we get to know each other a bit more before we start talking about marriage? When he finished speaking, Vincent told me not to take his word for it and encouraged me to seek God regarding our lives together. He was confident God would reveal His plan to me.

You could only imagine the thoughts that flooded my mind after that conversation. I was hesitant to ask God at first, but I wanted and needed to know if Vincent was indeed the man I would marry. I didn't want to miss what God had for me because of my fears, insecurities, and past experiences. In some ways, I thought that I would have to wait for many more years before God would trust me with a spouse because of my past.

I mustered up enough courage to asked God if Vincent was "The One." I prayed and readied my pen and paper next to my couch before falling asleep to record everything the Lord would speak. There was an expectation in my spirit that I would hear from God. But I had no idea where it came from. It had to have come from God. I felt so unworthy and undeserving; there was no way God would do that for me. But, much to my surprise, God spoke to me very clearly.

The Lord woke me up around 2 am and began to tell me things about Vincent and his children. He told me not to fear, that Vincent was the man I would marry and that He was mighty in Vincent's life. Six months later, on July 14, 2007, we were married.

The encounter with God revealed His love for me and in me. Only a faithful, loving God could love so unconditionally. After that, I did not doubt that God loved me with all my flaws. God did not need my help with His plan. He already had the plan mapped out. I just needed to trust Him.

That day changed my life forever. I was so overwhelmed with joy and love; and it wasn't because the Lord told me about Vincent, but because He spoke to me. I thought to myself, there is no way God was going to speak to me. I mean why would He? After all the wrong I've done? Although, I repented for those things and was back on the right path I still dealt with the guilt, shame and regret. I felt so unworthy because I failed so many times. God showed me that His love and plan for my life was greater than my past traumas and failures. "He looked beyond my faults and meet my needs."

CHAPTER 11

IT'S NOT OVER

Vincent and I have been married for 13 wonderful years, but it feels like a lifetime. He is my best friend and my number one supporter. God used him to rescue me from the many burning buildings I kept starting or ran into. He covers me with prayer, security and God's unconditional love. I knew that our marriage was blessed by God for His use. Our closeness and love for one another is an added blessing or in lay-men terms, "icing on the cake."

When we met, we were both on a parallel track with God and destiny. Our heart desire was to do God's will, no matter what it took. After we wed in 2007, we worked together in ministry. We served on several committees and served our leaders. God began to show us that we had a gift to minister to leaders and to help restore and strengthen them along their journey. We engaged in spiritual warfare often, because of the many adversaries that tried to stop the plan of God for our lives.

In, 2008, I had a vision from the Lord about going to Kentucky. My first thought was Lord is Kentucky on the map? I began to ponder other questions in my heart. What's in Kentucky? Are you sending us to connect with a couple in ministry there? I did not get as response from the Lord at that moment, so I shared it with Vincent, and we kept it before the Lord. Two, years later a door of employment opened for Vincent in Georgetown, Kentucky. We immediately thought about the vision. Could this the door to Kentucky? Vincent had his phone interview and was invited to a face to face interview; So he went. After he settled into the hotel he called me and said, "honey it feels like home." At that moment, I knew it was God. Vincent would not have said the country felt like home. In fact, I asked him if he would every consider moving to South Carolina and he gave me a strong NO! He was a city boy and needed all the noise that city life offered.

We received a release to move to Kentucky after Vincent received the job offer. We packed up our family in April 2010 and began our new journey. The transition was difficult because we left our entire families, two of our children and our first granddaughter in Philadelphia. Adjusting wasn't easy for our three daughters either. Making new friends and facing racism was challenging. We ensured them that God's plan was good for our family. In the tough times we were reminded of all the opportunities our children had been given in Kentucky that would not have been offered in Philadelphia.

As we walked in obedience, God began to add pieces to the puzzle regarding his plan to encourage us along the way. We birthed Restorer of Paths International Ministries in June 2010, only 2 months after moving to Kentucky. We ran into many people who were lost and looking for guidance, so we started to have bible study in our apartment. Shortly after we began to have Sunday worship service.

Before we left Philadelphia both Vincent and I had served in ministry as Elders, Prophets and Pastors. The shift to the new state was refreshing, but it wasn't long before I realized that I still had to be healed and set free in some areas. I was unaware that I had so many issues in my heart until I began to lead people on this new level. I was faced with an unusual spirit of fear, intimidation, comparison and jealousy. I realized I had very little emotions due to the wall I built to protect my heart and I prayed that God would help me feel again.

"Search me, O God, and know my heart:
try me, and know my thoughts:
And see if there be any wicked way in me, and lead
me in the way everlasting." Psalm 139:23-24

It was evident that poor self-esteem wasn't my only issue. Things were being revealed so that I could receive complete healing. There was no way for me to effectively lead people with so many unresolved issues. Vincent was very instrumental in my healing and deliverance process. He provided a loving, safe and secure place for me. When we married he was released by the Lord from the ministry that engaged in and taught spiritual warfare to come to the church I attended. God used him in the ministry of deliverance to bring me to a new level of freedom.

People emotional reactions to trauma can vary greatly and are significantly influenced by the individual's past. The reactions can surface in anger, fear, sadness, and shame to name a few. Just as I had problems identifying the affects the trauma had on my life; many individuals encounter the same difficulties.

I grew cold inside my heart unknowingly but desired to express true emotions with my husband and children. I wasn't taught how to express emotions in a healthy way as a child and on top of that, the trauma from my past kept me bound and numb. I knew something was terribly wrong when I could not be empathic to situations that required empathy and sympathy. There was no real grieving for me if someone was seriously hurt or passed away. I laughed at situations regarding my family that was not a laughing matter. My husband began to feel like I did not care and that I was closed off. He was concerned that I had no ability to respond at all let alone compassionately.

I shared with my husband one day that I was under demonic oppression and tormented with fear. He began to minister to me but felt that I needed to talk to our spiritual mother Apostle Lorraine Drake. He discerned that I needed a mother daughter connection and he was right. When I got her on the phone I began to cry like a waterfall. I cried like a child trying to explain what was wrong but was unable to communicate it due to the pain and the purging. Thank God, He knew what I needed and there was no need to explain. I was being delivered.

"Heartache purged layers of baggage I didn't know I carried. Gifts hide under the layers of grief." — Shauna L Hoey

Mom Drake let me cry until I could not cry anymore. She then walked me through my life by the power of the Holy Spirit and explained to me what was going on. She ministered to the little girl who was rejected, abandoned and abused; the teenage girl that had poor self-esteem, addictions and identity issues; the young lady that was trying to find her way but sabotaged herself by making poor decisions that led to bondage and being controlled by witchcraft.

"Healing trauma involves tears. The tears release our pain. The tears are part of our recovery. My friend, please let your tears flow."
— Dana Arcuri, Soul Cry: Releasing &
Healing the Wounds of Trauma

I am glad the Lord is all knowing and perfect in all His ways. He spoke to me through Apostle Drake and told me that He was going to heal my emotions at a steady pace because healing it at once would be too dangerous or will lead to feeling out of control. This was the beginning of another level of healing and freedom for me. The journey was painful at times but worth the promise.

Restored

God confirmed His forgiveness to me and revealed that I needed to forgive myself for my past mistakes so I could walk in freedom. Forgiving others was easier for me than forgiving myself. My sinful decisions cost me a great deal. In spite of the effects of trauma I needed to take responsibility for my action and how they affected the people that loved me. My relationship with my oldest daughter was shattered because of my lack of emotional and physical presence in her life. She became ill at the age of 18 which caused her to miss her graduation and prom. I became the blame for everything; even things I had no control over. After about 8-10 years our relationship was restored. She is no longer stuck in the past and is actually enrolled in college to complete her degree.

During my discovery journey, I faced great warfare, with myself and against the enemy. But I never stopped pressing, learning and growing. The enemy did not want me to know who God created me to be and that there was purpose in my pain. I realized that I could not pour into others what I didn't have. So, I draw close to God for refilling and my husband invested in a personal development program that provider more tools to help me discover my potential and how to lead others. I woke up one day and realized that I not only love myself but I actually liked who I had become.

Being aware of my dreams, personal values, talents, and personality gave me plenty of insight into my inner self. Many people end up defining themselves by relationships with others or the things they've always done, never considering the possibility of anything different. I encourage you to stop living in the shadow of your past and others. See yourself from God's perspective. Tap into your God given purpose. After all He gave it to you before you were born.

"Before I formed thee in the belly I knew thee; and before thou camest forth out of the womb I sanctified thee, and I ordained thee a prophet unto the nations." Jeremiah 1:5

Discovery

My lack of self-awareness cost me relationships and missed opportunities. Discovering my true identity and purpose has been challenging and yet fulfilling at the same. Breakthrough happened when I woke up one day and realized that I liked me in fact I actually loved myself, after hating everything about me for many years.

"So many people are not self-aware. They don't know how they show up or how they come across. They live so much In themselves they don't have a full view of what they do, have done and how it has impacted people or opportunities." — Dr. Matthew Stevenson

Without a clear idea about who you are or of the things that matter to you or the person you hope to become, you'll continue living for other people instead of yourself. I declare, today that you will no longer just exsist in life, but you will live in full awareness and assurance of who you were created to be. Remember you are not defined by what has happened to you or your current circumstances. Here are a few things to ponder and questions to ask as you begin your discovery journey.

1. What do I want from life?
2. Where do I see myself in 5 years? 10?
3. What do I regret?
4. What makes me proud of myself?

Explore your passions

- Passions help give life purpose and make it rich and meaningful. Maybe a passion for helping others guided you to the field of medicine, but your current position in medical billing doesn't quite fulfill your urge to provide compassionate care.
- Living out your passion might involve identifying the job you really want and researching the steps necessary for a career change. Or, maybe it's exploring ways to volunteer with your skills as a street medic.
- Think about what you spend your free time doing on a day-to-day basis. What excites you and brings joy to your life?
- Even interests like movies and music can offer insight. Taking some time to consider what you enjoy and look forward to most can help you discover ways to enrich your life.

Try new things

- Go to an Art Museum and learn about art-work and famous artist. *This was one of my favorite endeavor.*
- Check your local library or other community centers for free or low-cost adult learning classes.
- Exploring new hobbies. *I learned that I am really good at interior designing.*

Evaluate your skills

- Most people have a particular knack for something or other — crafting, home improvement, cooking, or any number of other skills. *I learned that cooking is not one of my favorite things to do. Pray for my family♭.*

- Gardening tips. If these skills are something you can picture yourself developing, why not put them into practice? *I don't have a green thumb and I am okay with that. I put fake plants out front.*

- Using your skills hones them, which can increase your confidence. Greater self-confidence, in turn, can encourage you to keep exploring these talents, along with any others you may not have noticed before.

Identify what you value about yourself

Your personal values, or the specific qualities you view as most important and meaningful, can tell you a lot about your nature. These values can help illustrate the life you want to live as well as the behavior you expect from others.

Values might include:

- honesty
- compassion
- loyalty
- creativity
- courage
- intelligence

Clarifying these values can help you make certain you're living them out. If you've never taken the time to explore what principles you find most valuable, making this part of your self-discovery process can have a lot of benefit.

Ask yourself questions:

- Why do I do the things I do?
- What drives me?
- What am I missing?
- What kind of impact do my choices have on the life I want?
- Then, apply these questions to all areas of your life.

Don't feel like you need to come up with answers immediately. Self-discovery takes time, and it's most helpful to carefully consider your responses instead of grabbing at the first thing that comes to mind. Above all, be honest with yourself. If you can't come up with a good answer, that doesn't mean you've failed. But it does suggest that some change might help.

Learn something new

- Learning works best when it's treated as a lifelong process.

- If you've always wanted to learn more about something in particular, take the time to study it. Books, manuals, or online tools can teach you quite a bit.
- Device Apps can help you get started learning anything like foreign languages. So if you have an interest, look it up — chances are good there's an app or free website dedicated to it.

Keep a journal

- If you kept a journal in adolescence, you might remember how it helped you explore your dreams and emotions. Picking up the habit of journaling (or blogging) again can help you get back in touch with yourself and learn more about the person you've become.
- A journal can help with self-reflection, but it can also serve a more practical purpose. You can use your journal to ask yourself questions and answer them, or explore any of the above tips more deeply.
- Journaling can also help you keep track of any patterns that keep coming up in your life. Learning more about unhelpful patterns can play an essential part in the self-discovery process. When you know what doesn't work, you can begin repairing it.

Talk to a therapist/counselor

- When the process of self-discovery seems overwhelming and you don't know where to start, therapy or counseling can provide a safe space to get some compassionate guidance.
- You don't need to experience mental health symptoms to benefit from professional support. Therapists help people sort through a range of issues, including goals clarification, career changes, and identity issues.

The process of self-discovery looks different for everyone, but it's generally not something that happens overnight. You do have somewhat of a jump start since you already know at least a little bit about yourself. But it still takes time and patience, just like getting to know someone else. Day-to-day priorities are important, certainly. But a life that's nothing more than a series of going through the same motions usually doesn't provide much enjoyment.

Today, one of my desires is to help little girls and boys identify how valuable they are, to believe in themselves and to build good self-esteem. God has a plan; and His plan is good despite one's childhood, race, circumstance, or economic status.

Vincent and I still reside in Georgetown Kentucky with 5 children, 2 sons-in-love and 11 grandchildren. We've helped strengthened and restored marriages, and ministry leaders. Restorer of Path International Ministries has been opened for ministry for 10 years. The Lord has graced us to disciple and train His children in Christian Living, Identity, Purpose, The Five-Fold Ministry, Spiritual Warfare, Deliverance and Spiritual gifts. We have blessed with an awesome ministry team that chose to be Chosen.

SUMMARY

One of the greatest lessons that I've learned, is that God uses everything to bring Him glory. Life's trials and tribulations of brokenness, struggles, failures and disappointments left me battered, bitter, confused and tormented. When I threw up my hands, the Lord encouraged me; when I held my head down, the Lord lifted it up; when I gave up all hope, His hope and love endured.

If you found yourself in any of the pages in this book, it is my prayer that you gain the courage and strength needed to defeat the traumas of your past. Your past does not define who you are. There is purpose in your pain. Coming to Jesus is the first step to learning who you are and complete healing.

For your enjoyment and encouragement, I've listed a few of my favorite scriptures that got me through to help you on your journey.

Scriptures I live by:

Romans 8:28
"And we know that all things work together for good to them that love God, to them who are the called according to his purpose."

Psalm 139:14
"I will praise thee; for I am fearfully and wonderfully made: marvellous are thy works; and that my soul knoweth right well."

Psalm 1

"Blessed is the man that walketh not in the counsel of the ungodly, nor standeth in the way of sinners, nor sitteth in the seat of the scornful. But his delight is in the law of the Lord; and in his law doth he meditate day and night. And he shall be like a tree planted by the rivers of water, that bringeth forth his fruit in his season; his leaf also shall not wither; and whatsoever he doeth shall prosper. The ungodly are not so: but are like the chaff which the wind driveth away. Therefore the ungodly shall not stand in the judgment, nor sinners in the congregation of the righteous. For the Lord knoweth the way of the righteous: but the way of the ungodly shall perish."

Philippians 4:6-8

"Be careful for nothing; but in every thing by prayer and supplication with thanksgiving let your requests be made known unto God. And the peace of God, which passeth all understanding, shall keep your hearts and minds through Christ Jesus. Finally, brethren, whatsoever things are true, whatsoever things are honest, whatsoever things are just, whatsoever things are pure, whatsoever things are lovely, whatsoever things are of good report; if there be any virtue, and if there be any praise, think on these things."

Philippians 1:6

"Being confident of this very thing, that he which hath begun a good work in you will perform it until the day of Jesus Christ:"

2 Timothy 1:7

"For God hath not given us the spirit of fear; but of power, and of love, and of a sound mind."

2 Corinthians 5:17

"Therefore if any man be in Christ, he is a new creature: old things are passed away; behold, all things are become new."

Isaiah 40:31

"But they that wait upon the Lord shall renew their strength; they shall mount up with wings as eagles; they shall run, and not be weary; and they shall walk, and not faint."

Psalm 46:10

"Be still, and know that I am God: I will be exalted among the heathen, I will be exalted in the earth."

Philippians 4:13

"I can do all things through Christ, which strengtheneth me."

Number 23:19

"God is not a man, that he should lie; neither the son of man, that he should repent: hath he said, and shall he not do it? or hath he spoken, and shall he not make it good?"

Psalm 34:1-4

"I will bless the Lord at all times: his praise shall continually be in my mouth. My soul shall make her boast in the Lord: the humble shall hear thereof, and be glad. O magnify the Lord with me, and let us exalt his name together. I sought the Lord, and he heard me, and delivered me from all my fears."

Psalm 34:19

"Many are the afflictions of the righteous: but the Lord delivereth him out of them all."

1 Corinthians 13

Though I speak with the tongues of men and of angels, and have not charity, I am become as sounding brass, or a tinkling cymbal. And though I have the gift of prophecy, and understand all mysteries, and all knowledge;

and though I have all faith, so that I could remove mountains, and have not charity, I am nothing. And though I bestow all my goods to feed the poor, and though I give my body to be burned, and have not charity, it profiteth me nothing. Charity suffereth long, and is kind; charity envieth not; charity vaunteth not itself, is not puffed up, Doth not behave itself unseemly, seeketh not her own, is not easily provoked, thinketh no evil; Rejoiceth not in iniquity, but rejoiceth in the truth; Beareth all things, believeth all things, hopeth all things, endureth all things. Charity never faileth: but whether there be prophecies, they shall fail; whether there be tongues, they shall cease; whether there be knowledge, it shall vanish away. For we know in part, and we prophesy in part. But when that which is perfect is come, then that which is in part shall be done away. When I was a child, I spake as a child, I understood as a child, I thought as a child: but when I became a man, I put away childish things. For now we see through a glass, darkly; but then face to face: now I know in part; but then shall I know even as also I am known. And now abideth faith, hope, charity, these three; but the greatest of these is charity.

CITED WORK

- **PUBLISHED IN HIGH PERFORMANCE, PHILOSOPHY, THINK WELL, VISION**
  REFLECTION, GRATITUDE AND BEGINNING A JOURNEY OF SELF DISCOVERY

- **9 Tips to Help You Kick Off Your Self-Discovery Journey**
  Medically reviewed by Alex Klein, PsyD — Written by Crystal Raypole on June 11, 2020

- The Holy Bible

CPSIA information can be obtained
at www.ICGtesting.com
Printed in the USA
BVHW090608230421
605636BV00010B/1866